The Black Girl Curriculum
10 Things Every Black Girl Should Know

by Ebony Janice Moore

BelleNoire Publishing, Inc.
Decatur, Georgia 2010

All rights reserved. No part of this work may be reproduced without permission from the author; any quotations must acknowledge the source. Nikki Giovanni "Ego Trippin" (c)1968 used with permission.

Table of Contents

Introduction: Get Free Girl/ Who Do You Think You Are?	5
Chapter 1: History of The Black Girl	13
Chapter 2: What Do You Call Yourself	20
Chapter 3: I Am My Sisters Keeper	26
Chapter 4: Your Temple is Not a Play Thing	32
Chapter 5: I am the Community	37
Chapter 6: What About Your Friends	42
Chapter 7: Is My Hair too Nappy	48
Chapter 8: Boys Will Be Boys	54
Chapter 9: Peer Pressure	63
Chapter 10: Gifts Are Gifts	67
Conclusion: Be The Change	72

Introduction

The Black Girl Curriculum came to me several years ago when one of my younger girl cousins was going through a phase in her life, clearly acting out, that required some kind of guide that did not exist for us (her community) or her. I thought about a series of conversations that I would have liked to have had with her prior to getting to this point. As I began to journal about a lot of the conversations I pondered on – The Black Girl Curriculum was born.

It seems very easy to give my younger cousin all the credit for the drama that inspired these thoughts… but during that same time I too was experiencing a lot, relationally, that demanded some serious introspection. While this thought process didn't always lead me to the "right" answers – these conversations surely took me to some questions I had never asked of myself before.

Who are we kidding? We are a mess. We come to this earth with clear instructions on what we are to do and who we are to be and then life happens and it's as if we lose every thing that God whispered in our ear before placing us in our mother's womb. What's kind of sad about that is – we may never recall or know all of those lost truths about ourselves (until we get to Heaven). The exciting thing about that is – this life is all about finding the questions and searching for the answers. Surely all of these answers are found in Christ Jesus. You know that! I know that! But do we really know that? If we did we would walk in that truth. Right?

Right!

The Black Girl Curriculum does not boast to be a list of complete questions/conversations that should be had with the young black female – but surely this is a place to start. As with my younger cousin's issues that lead to this thought process – and my own as well – I never intended to tell her what to do about her situations… only get her to thinking of all of the things about herself that she clearly had forgotten. "You are the head and not the tail." "You are above and not beneath." "You are the lender and not the borrower." "You are VERY good!" "You were created in the image of the only living God."

I do not claim to be an expert on the Black Girl. I'm still maneuvering through life myself. But – the fact of the matter is… anyone claiming to be an "expert" on people (period) is lying. We're all in this together. We are all daily learning things about ourselves that yesterday seemed impossible or unclear. Hopefully, we are allowing these insights to stretch us and strengthen us.

While I'm not an expert on the Black Girl, I am a black girl. A learning, loving, honesty is the best policy believing, true self seeking, God fearing sister girl that is blessed with "grace" in the area of relating with my sisters. I have a heart for the plight of the black girl and her sister and her cousin and her aunt, mother and grandmother. As a member of the Black Girl Community I am confident that it is not just my responsibility, but a part of my purpose on this planet to share as much of myself with black girls as possible.

More than anything – I pray these conversations help her get free!

Who Do You Think You Are?

Before we move any further, stop and ask yourself: "Who am I?" It is more important for you to assess this for yourself before you move any further through this discovery experience because then and only then can you begin to weed out the untruth's you've allowed yourself to believe and strengthen the areas of truth that you have found a way to hold on to.

Introduction Exercise
Who Do You Think You Are?

Take a moment to write down your first thoughts on this question. Be as honest as possible. What is the first thing that comes to your mind when I ask you this question? Whether good or bad, write your answer below:

_____
_____
_____
_____
_____
_____
_____
_____
_____
_____
_____

When I ask myself this question I always picture me dancing, spinning, twirling and free. That's who I am in my most pure state. I am just a free girl. My freedom is found in every portion of my life. My choices are made based on the fact that I am free. This means I make my own choices – I NEVER allow anyone else to convince me to do something that doesn't feel right to me.

My appearance is wrapped up in my freedom. I am daily teaching myself that how I look is the way that God wanted me to look. He said it is very good and so I don't have to add anything or take anything away from my physical self to make it any better. My relationships even reflect my freedom. No matter how much I love someone or care for some one… no person has the right to try to hold me in bondage. I do not allow my relationships to enslave me or cause me to think of myself contrary to what God said about me. When this gets to be the case – I have to take a step back and ask God to help me make the right choices in that particular relationship that will continue to reflect my freedom in Him. My worship is a clear indicator of my freedom. When

I am worshiping the Lord I have my hands raised high, my head thrown back and my eyes closed tightly. Nothing else matters but these intimate moments with God. I am free! I want to thank him and love him in action for giving me this freedom.

Because I see myself as a Free Girl, everything about me speaks to that.

Think about how you answered the above question.
Did you respond negatively about yourself or positive?
Negative _____
Positive _____

If your initial thoughts were negative, ask yourself why? Continue to ask yourself this question every day for the next week. Journal your thoughts, both on "Who Do You Think You Are" and also continue to journal your thoughts on why you answered negatively when prompted to be honest about yourself.

Did you answer negatively because you do not see yourself as good? Did you answer negatively because you do not believe all of the great things that God said about you? Did you leave the positive things out because they are overshadowed by the bad? What other reasons did you think negatively first? Is this the way your thought process normally works? Negative first?

If your initial thoughts were positive, ask yourself why? Continue to ask yourself this question every day for the next week. Journal your thoughts, both on "Who Do You Think You Are" and also continue to journal your thoughts on why you answered positively when prompted to be honest about yourself.

Did you answer positively because you only see yourself as good? Did you answer positively because you only believe the good things about yourself? Did you leave anything out that could use some work? Do you ever fail to see the big picture that you may have some things that need work? Is this the way your thought process normally works? Positive first?

*My response:

I answered the way I did because I am, in general, a glass half full kind of girl. That means, I can see the positive in just about any situation. This is a behavior that I have trained myself and prayed about long and hard over the years. I want to see myself the way that God sees me so when I think of myself, before I start talking about the extra weight I've picked up over the years, or the length of my hair and how I wish it were a little longer, or the blemishes on my chin, or even about the slight gaps in my teeth – I think of the things I consider "Good" first and then I go from there.

Don't get me wrong. I'm not always positive. I have days when I just do not see myself the way that God sees me. In fact, there is rarely a day when I am walking in 100% of my authority and greatness (one of my mentors, Katrice Mines, calls this My Black Girl Power), but "Glass Half Full" rather than "Glass Half Empty" is the way I'd rather see things. When I see myself in this light "First" it helps to minimize the lies I tell myself that merely tear me down, rather than encouraging and lifting me up.

When I'm really honest and I dig a little deeper, I can mention my anger issue. I can never leave out the fact that I allow my emotions to control me more than I would like. I can be selfish some times. I have many moments when I would love to make the world believe that "It's All About Me." I'm still learning how to share my space with others. And I can act kind of spoiled from time to time because I'm the youngest child.

Is this who I am? Absolutely NOT! God did not say these things about me, but that does not change the fact that I need to deal with these issues. Our goal as Christians is to try to be more and more like Him daily. That's going to take a lot of work and being honest with myself is the first step.

The purpose of this conversation is to engage black girls in internal dialogue. Before I can tell you about how great, grand, wonderful and marvelous you are – you have to deal with yourself and begin asking yourself questions that will move you closer to the truth of your greatness. A part of maturing is self assessment. If you aren't asking yourself the tough questions – no amount of praise and no activity is going to get you free.

Introduction Devotional
Who Do You Think You Are?

I remember being put on punishment as a young girl and being confined to my room. This was the worst kind of punishment for me because I loved to go outside and play with my friends. I loved to jump fences and swim. I loved to skip rocks at the bay and pretend to be a great inventor in the garage. My parents clearly saw this about me, and therefore – more than anything, my punishments usually involved me losing the freedom of running, skipping and jumping around outside.

One time I was on punishment and I looked outside, only to see all of my friends in a big huddle talking and laughing about something. I HAD to know what was going on out there. So I got my McDonald's Happy Meal "Halloween Edition" Pumpkin Face bucket, tied one end of a piece of string to the handle of the bucket and the other end of the string, I tied to the bunk bed and I hung it out of my window on the side of the house.

This particular window was hidden by a tree that had two huge limbs that you could stand on. Because the windows of our house were pretty high, you had to step into the opening between these two limbs to get to my bedroom window. I placed pieces of scrap paper and a pencil in the bucket and the next day, told all of my friends about my bucket. They could come step up in the tree, write notes on the paper in the bucket and then later on that night I'd open up the window and pull the bucket inside and read all of the day's events.

Even though it wasn't the same as being outside, some part of me felt fulfilled by my Secret Message Bucket because my parents weren't able to completely take away my freedom of "knowing."

When God placed me on this Earth, clearly "FREE GIRL" is something He said about me because even at that young age I knew that I HAD to be Free By Any Means Necessary. There are so many other stories of my childhood that speak to this need for freedom. That mentality has followed me all of my days and when I think of "Who Am I?" I can't help but to mention, first, "Free Girl!" because it is what is in me and always has been.

"Whom the Son sets free is truly free indeed!"-John 8:36

Are you a Free Girl?

Dear Heavenly Father,

I pray for my sister today. Lord, hear her heart. She wants to know more about who she is. She is hungry for this truth and desperate for your voice. Please let her know that she will only find the answer to this question in you. Allow her to be so committed to finding herself that along the way she realizes that an identity that doesn't include you is a pretty sad one. Whisper your Truths about her in her ear and remind her of how much you love and adore her. Show my sister that she is Free INDEED!

In Jesus' Name,

Amen

Intro Journal Entry
"Who Do You Think You Are?"

I am the apple of God's eye… (Zechariah 2:8) That means something.

Chapter #1
History of the Black Girl

I was in the third grade when the episode of "A Different World" that changed my life first aired. Imagine that, 8 years old and a television show was changing my life. In this particular episode Kim is upset that Whitley wants to display "Mamee" images and figurines at the Dorm Dedication Ceremony for Gilbert Hall. Kim replays a scene in her mind from her childhood where she dressed up as an African Queen for a Costume Contest at her school for Halloween and won. When her principle declared her the winner, he announced her as Aunt Jemima, the famous "Mamee" character on the syrup bottles instead of an African Queen. This left the young Kim distraught and as an adult, she carried this hatred of "Mamee" in her heart. At the end of the episode, after she has come to terms with the role of "Mamee" in her history as a black girl, Kim performs a piece by Nikki Giovanni, called Ego Trippin'. (*READ THIS POEM OUTLOUD AND THEN DISCUSS!)*

>I was born in the congo
>I walked to the fertile crescent and built
>the sphinx
>I designed a pyramid so tough that a star
>that only glows every one hundred years falls
>into the center giving divine perfect light
>I am bad
>
>I sat on the throne
>drinking nectar with allah
>I got hot and sent an ice age to europe
>to cool my thirst
>My oldest daughter is nefertiti
>the tears from my birth pains
>created the nile
>I am a beautiful woman
>
>I gazed on the forest and burned
>out the sahara desert
>with a packet of goat's meat
>and a change of clothes
>I crossed it in two hours
>I am a gazelle so swift
>so swift you can't catch me
>
>For a birthday present when he was three
>I gave my son hannibal an elephant

He gave me rome for mother's day
My strength flows ever on

My son noah built new/ark and
I stood proudly at the helm
as we sailed on a soft summer day
I turned myself into myself and was
jesus
men intone my loving name
All praises All praises
I am the one who would save

I sowed diamonds in my back yard
My bowels deliver uranium
the filings from my fingernails are
semi-precious jewels
On a trip north
I caught a cold and blew
My nose giving oil to the arab world
I am so hip even my errors are correct
I sailed west to reach east and had to round off
the earth as I went
The hair from my head thinned and gold was laid
across three continents

I am so perfect so divine so ethereal so surreal
I cannot be comprehended except by my permission

I mean...I...can fly
like a bird in the sky...

Imagine someone telling you at eight years old that you could fly like a bird in the sky! "How is this possible?" "Am I as amazing as this poem suggests?" "Am I so Hip that even my errors are correct?" At the age of 8 years old I had resigned in my heart that Nikki Giovanni was absolutely correct. And being a black girl in my predominately white town went from being awkward and slightly uncomfortable to exciting and liberating. No longer was I the random black girl in the class full of white girls with "beautiful long hair and blue eyes." I was now the young black girl that was clear that she was the descendant of kings and queens. Now I was the young black girl that carried a certain confidence inside because I was proud of this rich history.

While the "Mamee" character may not be the part of our history that we boast about most, even at a young age I was proud of the nobility, honor and integrity of my ancestors. Something about knowing how great, grand, and marvelous they were moved me in my soul to live up to that rich heritage and history. Honoring our ancestors by acknowledging our history is the only way for us to move forward and be everything that God called us to be. Our Heavenly Father is the King of Kings and we are His children – so that makes us of royal lineage no matter what color our skin is. However, our direct blood descendants were Kings and Queens. That makes us royal no matter how you look at it.

Yes, people of African descent were stolen, sold, and forced into slavery, but these were strong willed – never fainting – never dying – unyielding and unwilling to wave the white flag of defeat kind of people. That kind of resilience lives inside of you. You aren't just a direct descendant of Kings and Queens, great rulers, and history makers. You ARE a Queen, a great leader, and a history maker. You MUST look to your past to see yourself clearly today. You MUST look to your past to understand why the Father said everything He said to you about your future.

What negative thoughts about your history have you held onto that may be holding you captive?

Exercise #1
The History of the Black Girl
Research a black woman in history that you admire. Read a book about her or written by her. Learn more about this woman. Where is she from? What did she do to make her famous? What did she do that moved you even if she is not famous? What characteristics does she possess that makes her a great role model? How can you honor her in your every day life? Write about this black woman in history that you admire in your journal. Be sure to think, seriously, about the fact that anything that she accomplished, you have the ability to accomplish as well.

Name of Woman In History
you chose to study/research: _____

What did she accomplish? _____
_____
_____
_____
_____
_____
_____

What steps did she take to accomplish her goals? _____
_____
_____
_____
_____
_____

What do you want to accomplish in life? _____
_____
_____
_____

What steps must you take to accomplish your goals? _____
_____
_____
_____

16

Devotional #1
The History of the Black Girl

I played basketball in the 7th and 8th grade and I absolutely loved it! Even though the city that I am from is predominately white, the majority of my basketball team in both 7th and 8th grade was black. This isn't uncommon, but I point it out for the story I'm about to tell.

When I was in the 8th grade I experienced some of the most horrific racism that any young teen girl can ever experience. I remember traveling to an away game with my team to an all white school. When we got off the bus, a group of white boys started throwing snow balls at us. You would have thought that we wouldn't have gone any further than that, but instead we played the game any way.

The referee's were calling every thing in the other team's favor, no matter how right or wrong their calls were. On top of that, when we scored their whole school would stand up and boo. In the second quarter, I was mid air coming down from snatching up an offensive rebound when #45 from the other team bit me on my shoulder. I was outraged. I dropped the ball and grabbed my arm, expecting the referee that was standing right there to blow his whistle – but he never did and it looked as if the game was just going to continue.

Luckily, my coach finally realized that this was not a game we could continue. We forfeited the game. On our way out of the school the same group of boys from earlier that were throwing snow balls at us yelled after us, calling us "Monkey's" and "the N word." I was able to point out two of the boys when later questioned by school authorities and the two of them, along with #45 that bit me, were all expelled from school.

Unfortunately, this wasn't my last experience with this kind of hatred, but it was absolutely a learning experience for me. I was distraught after this happened. An emotionally drained 13 year old, confused and afraid of a world where people would judge me based on the color of my skin. "How could this be?" "Don't they realize how amazing I am? How beautiful and wonderfully made my people are?"

However devastating this particular experience was, oddly enough, it taught me compassion, patience and grace. Clearly those kids were only acting out of the ignorance that they had learned from somewhere. Generally that's where hate comes from. It's a disgusting learned behavior. Point blank period – it's ignorant. Rather than continue to perpetuate this hate back and forth, I quickly had to learn some things about myself to make me strong enough to handle this kind of situation, should it rear its ugly head again (and it has.)

Rather than fight hate with hate I decided to armor myself with love, patience and knowledge. Because I know that I am of royal descent both spiritually and in the natural – it's not too much anyone can say about me, or any ridiculous name that someone can call me that will make me change my mind about how I feel about myself. It's with this knowledge that I am equipped to teach tolerance in the face of ignorance and empower people with love in the face of hate. I often ask myself the question, "What would the King do?" Some times I am referring to Martin Luther King Jr., most times I'm talking about Jesus!

"My people perish for lack of knowledge." – Hosea 4:6

Dear Heavenly Father,

Thank you for your wisdom and insight. Your ways are perfect. Teach us to walk in your truth and only your truth. Help us to realize how special and unique you made us and give us the sense to not hate each other for those differences. Lord, how can we say we love you when we've never seen you, but we can't even love each other that we see each and every day? We need your help to make it day to day. Thank you for our past. Thank you for our present. Thank you for our future. We know the truth of who we are will always lead us back to you. Help us to embrace every part of ourselves.

In Jesus' Name,

Amen

Journal Entry #1
The History of the Black Girl

"You are a chose generation, a royal priesthood, an holy nation, a peculiar people." - 1 Peter 2:9

Chapter #2
What Do You Call Yourself?

I was named after both of my grandmothers. My name is Ebony Janice. My mother's mothers' name is Emma Jane. My father's mothers' name is Bernice. Hence – Ebony Janice (Janice sounds like Bernice). My aunt, who apparently at the time was very into all things "Black" thought Ebony would be a good name for me. Looking back, I often wonder if she really knew how powerful a statement she was making when she named me Ebony?

The literal translation of my name is "Black" (Ebony) "Gift from God" (Janice). Because "Black" went through this amazing shifting in the 1980's where "Black is Beautiful" was the slogan for all things "Black" I tend to keep "Black" synonymous with "Beautiful." Therefore I translate my name as "Beautiful Black Gift From God." I act just like it too! A "Beautiful Black Gift From God" that is…

Because my name is Ebony Janice and I act like an Ebony Janice, I am always having the conversation with myself about names and what I call myself and what I allow others to call me. I think, while our parents think they are just giving us names that are cute and nice, they are really declaring something over us that we will walk with forever and ever. I think about what else my name could have been and I can never come up with anything because I Am Ebony Janice!

You do know that the power of life and death are in the tongue? (Proverbs 18:21) So what you say or what you call a thing is not "just" words. What you say out of your mouth has the power to bring life. What you say out of your mouth has the power to bring death. What others say about you has the power to bring life. What others say about you has the power to bring death. Do you allow people to call you "LIFE," or do you allow people to call you "DEATH?"

People call you "LIFE" when they call you by the name that your mother gave you. People call you "LIFE" when they compliment you with nicknames that reflect your good character and your great attributes. People call you "LIFE" when they say things about you that are encouraging and uplifting.

People call you "DEATH" when they call you by names that your mother did not give you. "Bitch" and "Hoe" are NOT your name. Do not answer to it. "Hey Girl!" is NOT your name. Do not answer to it. "Fat, stupid, slut, tramp, whore, ignorant, lazy, no good, trifling, ugly…" None of those are your name. Do not answer to them.

Every now and then, I don't act like an Ebony Janice. I'm not being the Beautiful Black Gift From God that I was designed to be. I start procrastinating and answering to "LAZY." I even slip up and answer to "Not Good Enough" every now and then. I can be honest enough to tell you that in the past I've had the nerve to answer to a few of those other names above. But, remember I said – this life isn't about being an expert or even being perfect the first time around. This life is about a constant assessment and realization that much work is required.

Hopefully daily I'm becoming more and more like my heavenly father. In order for me to do that, I must think about what I allow others to call me. We call Him Savior because He Saves. We call Him Healer because He Heals. We call Him Jesus because He IS the CHRIST. Again, we must mirror this by only allowing others to call us by our name.

Your name is "LIFE!" Do not let anyone call you anything else but "LIFE!"

Exercise #2
What Do You Call Yourself

What is your name?

_____

Write down all of your nick names.

_____   _____

_____   _____

_____   _____

What does your name mean?
_____

If your name does not have a given meaning, write your own definition below:

_____

What do your nick names mean?

_____   _____

_____   _____

_____   _____

Write down who calls you each of these names in the corresponding spaces below.

_____   _____

_____   _____

_____   _____

Devotional #2
What Do You Call Yourself

I was raised in a home day care. One of the children at my mothers day care was a godsister of mine named Najaree. I thought this little girl was the most beautiful little girl I'd ever seen. I was in high school when she started coming to my mother's day care but I spent a lot of time in the summer and after school with the children. I started calling Najaree "Beautiful." I didn't just call her beautiful – as in describing her or telling her that she was beautiful. I literally renamed her "Beautiful." I called that little girl "Beautiful" so much that people often heard me call her that in public and asked, "Is that her real name?"

Even though I was just a teenager, I was very aware of the impact this was having on this little girl. Her big brown eyes, always seemed a bit brighter when her new name was appropriately called out. When I would ask her what her name was she would even reply, "Beautiful" most times.

Of course Najaree has grown up to be a very beautiful young lady in her teens, but as the years have gone by I'm sure she has forgotten the time that her older godsister renamed her "Beautiful" because that's exactly what she is.

I hope Najaree knows how amazing she is. I'm not there to tell her every day that she IS "Beautiful" but I pray that the seed was sown and watered and grows into truth for her. I expect the same of each of you reading this. I encourage you to embrace your name. If it's a creative, undefined, name that your parents made up – define your name yourself. You have that ability. You can say right now today – my name means "Destined For Greatness." So every time someone calls your name they are yelling, "Hey – Destined For Greatness… Come here!" When you answer to that you are essentially saying, "Yes, I am Destined For Greatness, how may I help you?"

Similar to the LIFE in calling Najaree "Beautiful" every day, you have power and authority to change the names that you've called yourself and allowed others to call you for years. No longer will you answer to "Death!" You shall LIVE and NOT DIE!

Dear Heavenly Father,

My little sister wants to live and not die. She's allowed her so called home girls to call her names that you did not ever intend for her.

Remind her of the good name that you gave her. Remind my little sister that you called her friend. Help her to understand that she was made in your image – she is NOT junk. Love her through this season of her life as she reclaims her name, her reputation and all of the other things that she allows others to say about her. Clean up her dirty, wicked places and make her pure so that she can stand worthy of the good name you have given to her.

In Jesus' Name,

Amen

Journal Entry #2
What Do You Call Yourself

"The Mouth of a righteous man is a well of Life."- Proverbs 10:11

Chapter #3
I Am My Sisters Keeper

I was too young to know anything about the infamous Freaknik that "terrorized" Atlanta back in the day... long, long before I was able to even understand what a "Freaknik" was. But, as a current resident, and especially with the recent revival of this unfortunate event in Atlanta, Georgia – I've heard many horror stories about Freaknik. One particular story is about a young freshman in college in Birmingham, Alabama that took a trip to Atlanta with her girlfriends, probably just curious to find out what "Freaknik" was all about. All of her girlfriends had gotten drunk, but she had decided not to drink. She wasn't necessarily there for that kind of party. She just wanted to hang out – see the city and enjoy herself as much as she could without regretting her decisions when she returned to school.

A group of guys approached her on the street one night, walking with her inebriated "friends" and told her to dance for them. When she said no, they started ripping off her clothes. Her drunk girl friends couldn't do anything because they were too far gone in their drunken stupor to be of any real assistance. This young lady was stripped until she was bare naked and then beaten in the streets of Atlanta, Georgia.

As if, being stripped naked and beaten in the streets wasn't enough, her girlfriends, once sober, blamed her for the incident stating that she must have been being her normal "stuck up" and "uptight" self. Clearly these girls were not her real friends and while being stripped and beaten was not her fault, the major mistake that she made was in not surrounding herself with other women from her community that understood the need to make wise and safe choices, both for themselves and for her.

To add insult to this story, other girls, that did not know her, stood around and watched this happen. Who is the woman that would stand back and watch another woman being beaten and dehumanized? I listened to young girls make very horrifying comments after singer Chris Brown beat his, then girlfriend, Rhianna. "She probably deserved it." "She probably started it." "She didn't deserve him anyway." What kind of young ladies are we raising as a community when this is the mindset of our teens?

No matter what, no woman deserves to be abused physically, mentally or emotionally. Furthermore, it is my responsibility to ensure that you are treated the way you deserve to be treated as a child of God and it is your responsibility to ensure that I am treated the way I deserve to be treated as a child of God. We belong to each other. No longer can we stand to the side and allow our sisters to be beaten down by the ugly ways of society. If no one else EVER takes the time to affirm us – we must affirm ourselves.

Furthermore, how can I walk past my own reflection and not acknowledge it? Sister – you ARE me and I AM you. We belong to each other and with out the other, we could not continue to exist. I have personally vowed to NEVER let any of my sisters be treated like less than the royal Queen that she is because when she is abused I am too. That is just how much we are connected. I am absolutely My Sisters Keeper.

Exercise #3
I Am My Sisters Keeper

With a group of girls, sit down and discuss the following:

Where is the love?

For ourselves:

For each other:

For our elders (older black women):

Where is the respect?

For ourselves:

For each other:

For our elders (older black women):

What are your needs from your sister?

What does it mean to be a reflection of your sister?

Do you ever walk past the clear reflection of yourself and not acknowledge it?

What is the most important issue that needs to be resolved that will help you to become closer to your sisters?

What are you doing to assure your sisters that you are there for them?

Devotional #3
I Am My Sisters Keeper

I have always had many girlfriends. From my childhood on through my adulthood – I've had a pretty good understanding that my relationships with other women were not only necessary but mandatory. I did, however, go through a brief stage of having male friends that I was very close with. I think a lot of us go through this stage, "I'm just cooler with guys. They have less drama. I can't really get along with girls that well." Is that not the most foolish mess you have ever heard?

Of course that stage in my life, because I'm way too much of a sister girl, was VERY brief. I've maintained the majority of my close girlfriend relationships from childhood (my best friend Jessica Ralph and I have been friends since elementary school – going on 20 years of friendship) and I am one of the main women in my family that makes an extra special effort to affirm the others. I just love my sisters!

My freshman year of college, I was blessed to become friends with a group of young women that remain an absolute MUST in my life. Shawntele Willis (now Shawntele Star), Dawnielle Willis (now Dawnielle McIntosh) and Belinda Joyce Styles became close to me – like blood sisters – during a time when I needed girlfriends the most and my life will never be the same because of them.

Belinda and I were very similar in that we had a group of guy friends that we hung out with – but we were both clearly crying out for some Christian female relationships that would speak to who we were and where we knew we were going. We were the loners just going to class, doing our school work, and being involved on campus. We didn't cause trouble – we didn't bother anyone. This was our clear draw to one another. Shawn and Dawn, were those girls that came on campus and everyone immediately had something negative to say because they were so pretty and dressed so nice. Being twins did not help their case either. There is a story told that once, they marched for more than a mile in the Martin Luther King Jr. Day celebration in stiletto heels. Who wouldn't hate that kind of girl? Belinda and I... that's who!

The reality is, these two girls, just because of the way that they carried themselves, took a lot of heat and got a lot of drama for just being beautiful girls. They were called "snobs" and "stuck up" but they were the farthest thing from that. I think Shawn and Dawn are quite possibly, two of the most genuine young women I've ever met. When we became friends, of course, I got the chance to get to know them both beyond the great hair and the amazing wardrobe. They are hilarious, witty, and extremely intelligent and none of the negative things that people had to say about them.

Once, during our sophomore year, this guy that I was interested in tried to hit on Shawn when I wasn't around. Let's just say, after she got through with him – he NEVER thought about testing the boundaries of our friendship again. I'm grateful for girlfriends that reflect the kind of love for me that I have for them. I'm blessed to have a group of friends that always call me on my mess and uplift me in and out of season. I trust these women, like sisters, and I'm confident that they will always be a part of my life. We strive to exemplify sisterhood and make every effort to share our friendship as a form of ministry to others.

Dear Heavenly Father,

Thank you for the women that you have put in my life for a season and for a lifetime. Help me to always be encouraged by them and to feel their love for me. When I need to show them compassion – remind me of how "imperfect" I am. When I need to uplift them, give me the courage and the boldness to say just what you would have for me to say. Thank you for making each and every one of them. Help me to give them the kind of relationship they need to make it another day. Help them to be for me who I need them to be to make it another day. Remind us that we ARE sisters in Christ and we MUST keep each other.

In Jesus' Name,

Amen

Journal Entry #3
I Am My Sisters Keeper

"And the Lord said unto Cain, Where is your brother Abel? And Abel said, I do not know, Am I my brother's keeper?" – Genesis 4:9

Chapter #4
Your Temple Is Not A Play Thing

How do you treat your body? Do you eat healthy? Do you exercise? How do you expect other people to treat your body? Do you allow men to make comments about your body parts? Do you expect certain things because of the way your body looks? What types of things to do you put into your body – through your ears? Your eyes? Your heart? Do you truly believe that your body is a temple? If so – do you treat it as such?

Exercise #4

Write down all of the things that you do NOT do to encourage a healthy and whole body (temple):

_____   _____

_____   _____

_____   _____

Write down all of the things that you do that encourages a healthy and whole body (temple):

_____   _____

_____   _____

_____   _____

My Responses:
Write down all of the things that you do not do to encourage a healthy and whole body (temple):
　Over eating　　　　　　　Missing Yoga Classes
　Eating too much junk food　　Not eating enough fruits and veggies
　Paying too much attention to the size of girls on television

Write down all of the things that you do that encourages a healthy and whole body (temple):
Dancing alot　　　　Yoga　　　　　Eating organic foods
　Shopping for fresh produce　　Defining my idea of beauty for myself
　Spending time journaling about my idea of a healthy body size

Exercise# 4 (continued)

Now write down all of the things you can do to start promoting a healthy and whole body (temple):

Eating healthier portions   Limit junk food intake
Sticking to a strict yoga schedule Go for longer walks
Eat more fruits and vegetables   Pray for more self confidence
Ignore the commercials with the size 2 models

Have you noticed yet that the majority of your change will require you to simply change your mind about something? If you do not exercise, all you have to do to change this is change your mind about exercising. You only get one body so make sure that you are treating the one you have with care and concern. If you allow men to say sexual things about your body parts, all you have to do to change this is change your mind about whether or not this is ok. Since it is not okay for men to talk about your body parts (I call this "Talking Underneath Your Clothes") then you will need to simply start praying for the boldness to stop them. If you do not eat healthy foods, all you have to do to change this is start today eating healthy foods.

Again, remember, your body is a Temple. It is holy and it is sacred. Most of all, it belongs to God and He only plans to give you one of them. Enjoy the body that you have by making wise, healthy and holy choices for your life.

Devotional #4
Your Temple Is Not A Play Thing

Erykah Badu is, and probably will always be, one of my favorite artists. I've thoroughly enjoyed her music from the beginning of her career and I feel like she just continues to grow as a musician, a singer and overall as a person. Even as much as I love her, however, I can not always get with what she's got going on. I could list some of the things I consider flaws – but he without sin cast the first stone.

What I will say is – the first time I saw her video for "Window Seat" from her most recent album: Return of the Ahnk, I can't say that I was necessarily moved. It was extremely controversial, of course, because Erykah literally filmed the video guerilla style as she walked down the streets of Dallas, music playing in the background, she stripped naked before you hear a shot fired and then see Erykah fall naked onto the ground. To me, it wasn't that deep. I simply thought *"Erykah is getting naked so she can boost those record sales.*

Part of the reason the video was so controversial is because she actually walked down the streets of Dallas and got naked in front of actual people – specifically children. A few days after the debut of the video, I read an article by a reporter that watched the video with her 6 year old daughter and then interviewed her after they viewed the controversial video together. This little girl has to be the epitome of "Amazing" because when asked, "Why do you think they shot her in the end," her response was, "Because she's beautiful and Free!" I was, of course, moved to tears. Maybe I had shot Erykah too, just because she was beautiful and free. I mean – I would NEVER do anything like that so surely she was WRONG for doing it. Right?

I took the time, after reading that interview to give the video another chance, and upon watching it this time with the expectation of getting something for myself, I realized that Erykah's body looks very similar to mine. She has a slim waist, thick hips, a round behind, and thick thighs. Then I started to think about the fact that this may have been the fist time I had EVER seen a black woman on tv with my body shape that wasn't being hyper-sexualized by the media. Either black women on tv are rail thin or morbidly obese. There are no average size black women that get to be the main character in the video, or in the movie or in the commercial that are being praised and celebrated as beautiful.

At the age of 27 years old, Erykah Badu walking down the street naked was my first time seeing "ME" on tv. Not that I would be walking down the street naked. My revelation wasn't even about that. It was about the fact that I finally didn't see myself in the back ground of the video popping my behind or gyrating to some raunchy lyric. This beautiful woman was stripping herself naked for the world to see all of her flaws and how amazingly beautiful that was.

I shared this story with some of the women from my church and one of them pointed out to me that God was really trying to show me something about myself in that area. I, immediately, knew what she was talking about. I have to be very transparent when I say that I have perpetuated the idea of mostly thinking of my own body, in an extremely sexual way for a very long time... so much so to the point that I've not always treated my body with the respect that I deserve as a child of God.

How can I go any further encouraging you with a curriculum designed specifically for your needs, if I am not honest enough to tell you that this curriculum has blessed my very own life. Constantly assessing who I am and who I believe God that I will become has kept me sane and even spared my life. It was a moment of introspection that lead me to the reality that *my body is a temple and not a play thing*. It was a moment of self assessment that taught me that I am beautiful and more than a mound of flesh on my back side. It was a moment of honest reflection that reminded me of the truth of what God said about me.

This body is my temple. I must honor it by being healthy and whole. I can't feed it the garbage that society tries to force down my throat. I can't allow the media, videos and ridiculous lyrics to songs to tear me down. And I absolutely can't cheapen the holiness of my body by playing into the music industries idea of me. I am MUCH more than some bump and grind movements. This body is my temple. I MUST treat it as such!

Dear Heavenly Father,

Thank you for using the simplest things to minister to our hearts. Thank you for making me whole and cleaning me up and that the mistakes I have made in the past are not who I am, they are just a part of my testimony. I am glad that you still see fit to use me even though I haven't always honored your temple as a holy sacred place. Please give my sisters the courage to make righteous choices for themselves that show you the proof of their obedience to your word. Please give them the boldness to declare that the weapons of lies and deceit that videos try to feed them will not prosper in their life. Allow the sins we commit with our body to become utterly sinful to us so that we will only choose righteousness.

In Jesus' Name,
Amen

Journal Entry #4
Your Temple Is Not A Play Thing

"What? Know ye not that your body is the temple of the Holy Ghost which is in you, which ye have of God, and ye are not your own? For ye are bought with a price: therefore glorify God in your body, and in your spirit, which are God's." – 1 Corinthians 6:19,20

Chapter #5
I Am The Community

If we lived on an island by ourselves, maybe service would not be as important as it is. But we do not. We share this earth with others that God created and our creation surely came with an expectation of serving. That's a basic part of our Christian walk. The fact of the matter is – I have something that you need and you have something I need. Just by being a part of any community, I am charged with the responsibility to give back and to pay it forward, I do not just serve my community. I AM Community Service!

My community is much more than just a group of people that share religion or culture in common – my community consists of every human being. When I start believing that I AM THE ONE that will make the difference – then my whole attitude about my surroundings will change. I Am The Community... What does that mean to you? How will that effect how you treat your neighbors? The person that you see walking down the side walk every morning? The bus driver? The homeless person on the corner?

Exercise #5

Along with another girl from your school, your church, your youth group, or your family – choose an issue that really gets under your skin and work together to come up with a realistic solution. If drunk drivers really bother you and every time you hear about a drunk driver you are moved emotionally... then choose drunk drivers as your issue. If your issue is teenage pregnancy and you have resigned in your heart that before you leave this earth you MUST do something about the fast increasing rate of teenage pregnancy then that is the issue that you should choose.

Next, meet the need! What problem in life are you the answer to? For example: I am always moved to tears when I see homeless children on the street. I don't have a house for all of them, but I do have some change for some food. I do have an extra coat at home. I do have information on where they can possibly go to stay and get a good nights sleep.

My Project:

The problem: Homeless Youth
The solution: Canned Food Drive for a local Shelter

Another Example:

When the hurricane almost engulfed Haiti, I was devastated. I thought about what the people that survived must be going through and how I could help. I started to think about things that I can't make it through the day with out. You know... the things you and I take for granted. Washing powder, fresh water, and clean underwear were the first things to come to my mind.

The problem: Uncomfortably unclean people
The solution: Send clean underwear to Haitian children and women

There are so many things that you can do. Start small – you never know what your Service Project could do for the life of another person. Don't worry about trying to feed, clothe, or save every person – changing the life of even ONE person will bless their life and change you forever!

Devotional #5
I Am The Community

I grew up in a very small town. I can say, with near certainty, that I either know every black person from my city or I know their family. That's not an exaggeration. Even though I am a city girl at heart, a great part of the benefit of growing up in the size town I grew up in is what I was taught about community.

When I was a young girl, I remember the kind of neighbors that would chastise you for being disrespectful or for "cutting up" and then tell your parents on you so that you would get in trouble for misbehavior twice. I remember having the kind of neighbors that could come up the street and ask to borrow a cup of milk or some sugar. I remember being allowed to spend the night at friends houses and not fearing older brothers or fathers touching young girls or being inappropriate. I remember my childhood friends parents taking me in after school to feed me or to watch out for me until my mother got off work. I remember feeling like I had family every where I went, because someone was absolutely always watching out for me.

To me – that is community! Since I've left my small town, that reality is one of the things I miss most about growing up there. I lived in Cincinnati, and other than my group of girlfriends, I never found the community of my childhood. I lived in Birmingham, Alabama and while there, even in the good old south, I never found the community of my childhood. Then I lived in northern Virginia, close to D.C., and I still never found the community of my childhood.

At some point, I had to decide for myself how important community was to me. The one thing in life that I decided that I would be unreasonable about is community. That simply means, I will not make any excuses or blame anyone else if I live in Atlanta, Georgia – or move around to a million more places – and never find the community that I am searching for.

That means I have to BE the community. I have to be the one that cares so much about other peoples children that I refuse to allow them to act out, especially when their parents aren't around. I have to be the one to offer my cup of sugar or my glass of milk. I have to engage my neighbors in conversation and get to know them while being vulnerable enough to let them know me. I have to foster that kind of communication that is necessary for a thriving community to exist. And

I have to promote diversity and tolerance so that no person feels isolated or left out in the community.

It is my responsibility to Serve my Community! How can I serve an unestablished community? It's impossible. So, first I am making every effort to daily acknowledge that I Am the Community. Next, I am rallying all of the people that are apart of my community by serving them. Lastly, I make sure to celebrate the beauty of my ever changing community as times swift transitions reveal the newness of what my community will be.

Dear Heavenly Father,

I am glad that you did not create me to be on this earth by myself. I enjoy the people that you have put into my life. I recognize that my family is not just my mother, father, sister, and brothers – but I am a part of an extended family called the Body of Christ and together we declare your glory. Please Lord, forgive us for not being for one another who you called us to be. It's reasonable that at the very least we could love one another. But sadly, we have failed at even that seemingly simple task. We need your presence and your power to walk in the truth that you said about us. Teach us how to serve others so that we can prove our love to you. For how can we say we love you whom we have never seen but we can't even love our neighbor that we see each and every day? Thank you for your community.

In Jesus Name,

Amen

Journal Entry #5
I Am The Community

"You, my brothers, were called to be free. But do not use your freedom to indulge the sinful nature ; rather, serve one another in love." - Galatians 5:13

Chapter #6
What About Your Friends?

When I was in middle school, a group by the name of TLC, came out with a song called, "What About Your Friends?" They asked, "What about your friends? Will they stand their ground? Will they let you down?" The song continued, after a couple of "yeah's" and "ooh's"… "What about your friends? Are they gonna let you down? Will they ever be around? Or will they turn their backs on you?"

These are some really great questions to ask of the people that you call "friend."

Exercise #6

Are your friends strong in their principles? (Will they stand their ground?_
Yes _____
No _____

If you said Yes describe the characteristics you think prove that your friends are strong in their principles:

If you said No describe the characteristics that you think prove that your friends are not strong in their principles:

Do you think this is an important factor in choosing a friend?
Yes _____ Why? _____

No _____ Why? _____

Are your friends always there for you? (Will they let you down?)
Yes _____
No _____

If you said Yes describe the characteristics you think prove that your friends are always there for you:

If you said No describe the characteristics that you think prove that your friends are not always there for you:

Do you think this is an important factor in choosing a friend?
Yes _____ Why? _____

No _____ Why? _____

What other characteristics do you think are important in choosing a friend?

Do you hang with only people that look like you?
Yes _____ Why? _____

No _____ Why? _____

Act like you?
Yes _____ Why? _____

No _____ Why? _____

Know the things that you know?
Yes _____ Why? _____

No _____ Why? _____

Or do you embrace all types of people?
Yes _____ Why? _____

No _____ Why? _____

Think about your best friend. Now answer these questions:

Is she/he mean to others?   Does she/he gossip?
Yes _____   Yes _____
No _____   No _____

Is she/he a bully?
Yes _____
No _____

Do other people have bad things to say about her/him?
Yes _____
No _____

Is she/he always a part of drama?
Yes _____
No _____

If you answered "Yes" to any of the above questions about your best friend – answer this next question:

Is this a reflection of you and how you treat others?

Yes _____

No _____

They say "Birds of a Feather Flock Together."

Each individual person that you call friend may have something unique to add to your life – so its good to not exclude "different' types of people. Its also good to note that EVERY person that you call friend may not necessarily be your Friend!

What is your definition of a friend?
_____
_____
_____
_____
_____
_____
_____

Devotional #6
What About Your Friends

I have been friends with Jessica Ralph since we were young girls. We were destined to be friends. We were born in the same hospital three days a part. Our families have known each other forever and ever. We lived right around the corner from each other through the majority of our elementary school years and we went to churches that were literally in walking distance from each other.

I was always fascinated by her big hair and her great smile (I still am) and she has always been fascinated by how free I am. We share a mutual respect for each other and in general I am confident she is smarter than me but for some reason she thinks I have all the answers! This affection and regard keeps us bound together in covenant and encourages us to continue to put in the kind of work it takes to remain friends.

However, we couldn't be any different if you painted me red and her green. While Jessica and I have been in each others lives for as far back as either of us can remember – we are two completely different characters. She is a "Thinker." I am a "Feeler." She is EXTREMELY career oriented. I place more importance on relationships! I MUST get myself a husband and some kids. She'd be happy with a boyfriend, maybe in some time a husband, and isn't thinking about children any time soon. She believes that distance makes the heart grow fonder. I need you to be right up the street or I'm going to have some problems.

The reason that Jessica Ralph is, and will always be my best friend, is that she reflects the best parts of me. I would absolutely with out a doubt be able to 100% answer no to all of the questions from the bottom of Exercise #7. Is she/he mean to others? NEVER! Does she/he gossip? Even when I want to – she refuses. Is she/he a bully? She got over her bully stage in the third grade. (I was the only one she "TRIED" to bully.) Do other people have bad things to say about her? If they do, I'm confident they have concocted these stories. Is she a part of drama? Jessica Ralph, in general, has always been the most drama free person I know.

The best parts of her and the worst parts of her speak to my heart and our differences and similarities are balanced just enough to keep us connected forever. A 20+ year relationship takes work. We have had our fair share of disagreements and what you would call "ups" and "downs." No matter what – we are both committed to putting forth the effort necessary to stay friends. When we get close to a "break up," we kick in to super communication mode and lots and lots of prayer.

It is rare to find a friend like the friend I have found in Jessica. She is one of the best parts of me, and I pray that I am a reflection of the best parts of her. I would be honored to say that "We <u>are</u> Birds of A Feather!"

Dear Heavenly Father,

Thank you for the friendships that you have placed in my life. Thank you for the wisdom required to choose the right friends and the insight required to stay friends. I pray for my little sisters, that they learn to make wise choices regarding the people they allow into their personal space. Dear Lord, remind them of your undying Love and allow them to know that because you called us friend, we can and should model our friendships after the friendship you have offered to us. Forgive us for being shallow and ignorant in our friendship choices of the past. Help us be bold in our friendship choices to come. We receive your love for us that you show through our friendships.

In Jesus' Name,

Amen

Journal Entry #6
What About Your Friends

"A man that has friends, must show himself friendly: and there is a friend that sticketh closer than a brother."-Proverbs 18:24

Chapter #7
Is My Hair Too Nappy?

Natural (unrelaxed/unprocessed) hair on black peoples head has commonly been referred to as "nappy". Good hair versus bad hair in the black community has always been a comparison of wavy/loose curls and tight kinky coils. Fortunately, more and more people are becoming educated on this subject. I have defined "Good Hair" as "Healthy Hair" as opposed to its culturally historic implications that have described "Good Hair" as hair that looks European. I'm proud to say that when I asked my boyfriend what he considers "Good Hair" he said – "Hair that doesn't break."

While "nappy" stems back far into and beyond slavery, black people have been struggling internally as a culture with the idea of "nappy for far too long. The reality is, its negative connotations within our community – no matter how many of us have embraced the term and endear it towards one another – have kept us paralyzed as far as our self identity and positive outlook on our outward appearance is concerned.

If you listen in on many black mothers while they are combing their daughters hair (if that hair is unrelaxed) you will often hear these mothers making a fuss about how "nappy" or "kinky" or "difficult" their daughters "natural" hair is to comb. Until very recently (within the past 5 or so years) natural, non chemically altering products did not exist to help parents comb through their daughters "naturally curly, wavy, or kinky hair." Because of the "fuss" that surrounds combing a black girls hair – young black girls have the tendency to grow up "fussing" with their hair.

For example: When I was a young girl, my mother relaxed (permed) my hair at an extremely early age. That was her choice – and while, as an adult I totally 100% wish that were not the case – in my 6, 7, 8 year old mind, I always knew when my hair was getting too "nappy" and it was time for a perm. My young mind had been trained to take note of my roots and as soon as the natural curl, kink or wave began to show up I was swooshed off to the hair salon or the kitchen table to get my no-lye relaxer smoothed over my head until it burned just enough to know it was working.

I was 21 years old when I decided to cut all of the relaxed hair out of my head and start growing my natural hair out. I don't remember my reasoning being some deep expression of my 'blackness' but I absolutely would never go back to relaxing my hair after seeing what my natural state is. I NEVER imagined that my hair really wasn't 'nappy' (of which I apparently had a negative perception of what "nappy" meant as well) – just curly. I have an extremely tight curl in fact. Just think – all of these years I thought of those curls as "negative naps."

To show you how much society has effected the way we think of "black hair" that is "natural" and "unrelaxed" there are people that still look at my hair and think it is not "Good Hair." It is strong, healthy, curly hair that grows out of my head faster than it ever did when I was putting chemicals on it for all of those years. How could that be "Bad Hair?"

People commonly refer to "Good Hair" as hair that most closely resembles European Hair. If I can be undignified for a moment Young Black Girl… Just because your hair looks more (quote, unquote) European does not make that "Good Hair." Just because your hair lays down bone straight, or your curls are more wavy and loose does not make that "Good Hair." While it is technically "Good Hair" if it is healthy growing hair, it's not "Better Hair" than the sister next to you with shorter, tighter curls, deeper waves, or seemingly unruly kinks.

You are unique and special. You are fearfully and wonderfully made. Your kinky, curly, wavy, rolling, dancing, jazzy hair that does what you want it to do and/or fights with you and is unruly and opinionated is YOURS. If you have decided to wear your hair relaxed – that's fine! Love your hair. Keep it healthy and conditioned, moisturized and trim your ends often. That's the way to promote "Good Hair." If you have decided to wear your hair natural – that's great too! Love your natural hair. Keep it healthy and conditioned, moisturized and trim your ends often. That's the way YOU promote "Good Hair."

Either way – the answer is NO! Your hair is absolutely, 100% NOT too nappy. It's "Good!" In fact… It's VERY Good!

Exercise #7

Sometimes hair can be a distraction from how beautiful you really are. You can get so caught up in what your hair looks like that you miss out on all of the other great attributes that you have. Take this time to write down kind words about each of the following parts of your body:

My feet are:

My eyes are:

My nose is:

My mouth is:

My hips are:

My chin is:

My skin is:

My teeth are:

My thighs are:

My head is:

My hands are:

My ears are:

My fingernails are:

Daily Devotional #7

When I was 24 years old I was diagnosed by my doctor with Polycystic Ovarian Syndrome (PCOS). This disease is caused by a hormonal imbalance that causes cysts to be formed on ovaries. It is a sickness that doctors have not found a cure for and most commonly subscribe medications that regulate the estrogen in the body so as to balance the hormones. Of course my doctor prescribed several medications that were supposed to regulate my body to counter some of the symptoms of the PCOS. Unfortunately, I instantly experienced some terrifying side effects from one of these medications and large patches of my hair started falling out. I was horrified.

Because of these huge patches in my head, there was nothing that I could do but cut my hair completely off. It was cut short into a fade like a boys hair cut. Prior to having to cut my hair off because of the medicine, I had a short afro, so the cut wasn't a drastic 12 inches or anything like that, but girls never want to HAVE to cut their hair off because it's falling out. It was devastating.

I had never worn a wig before but for some reason the first thing I thought when I left the barber shop was, "I need to go buy a wig!" I went an bought a wig that had curly hair. It wasn't a ridiculously long haired wig, but none the less, it was a wig. That weekend I was going to Washington, D.C. for the National Convention for the NAACP with my Aunt Phyllis. When I arrived, I had the wig on. She didn't say anything about it but I knew it was coming. I spent the first day wary about what people were thinking because I was sure every one knew I had a wig on.

That night in our hotel room my Aunt Phyllis asked me to let her see my head without the wig. I took the wig off and she looked at me for one quick second before saying, "You've never been more beautiful." Needless to say, I never put that wig back on. The very next day when I went back to the convention center for the day's session, everyone - from the construction workers on the street to the coffee vendor at the entrance - only had great things to say. I was this beautiful brown skinned woman with high cheek bones walking proud with my head held high. I was confident because I knew my aunt would not lead me astray.

What I learned in the experience of cutting my hair off that first time is that hair is such a distraction that you never really take the time to look at your face. Hair will cover your forehead. Hair will be big and fluffy on the top of your head so that people notice it more than they notice your eyes or your ears. We even style our hair in certain ways specifically to try to cover up things on our head or face that we consider flaws. Cutting my hair showed me that without hair I was still EbonyJanice and that all by itself is a beautiful thing.

My hair doesn't define me at all so I absolutely don't allow the texture of my hair or the length of my hair to determine how I feel about myself. I am beautiful, mostly because I am a good person. I am kind to people and I allow the goodness that is inside me to shine through. No length of hair, no wave and no curl will make you anymore lovable if you have nasty insides. So no... Your hair is NOT too nappy! Your hair is EXACTLY how it should be... Love it!

Journal Entry #7
Is My Hair Too Nappy

For everything God created is good, and nothing is to be rejected if it is received with thanksgiving. - 1 Timothy 4:4

Chapter #8
Boys Will Be Boys

If you are teenage girl reading this book, you probably have already experienced the shocking arrival of your menstrual cycle, also known as a Period. Make sure to talk to your parents or someone you trust when this comes. Do not be ashamed. Your menstrual cycle is not something to be ashamed of. It is a part of your design as a girl.

When your menstrual cycle comes – your hormones will probably kick into overdrive. There is NOTHING wrong with this either. Again, you should talk to your parents or an adult you trust about what you are feeling. What you absolutely do NOT want to do is act on everything that your body tells you it wants or craves at this time. These hormones can cause you to be emotional and those emotions may tell you that you must have a certain food. These hormones can also cause you to think you must be touched in certain places that unmarried young ladies should not be touched.

Again, there is nothing wrong with you for feeling the way you feel. However, discipline, obedience and wisdom will be required during this season of your life in order for you to make the kinds of lasting decisions that you won't regret later on down the road. I have said it several times at this point, I'll say it again: Talk to your parents or an adult you trust during this time. Even if it has already come prior to you reading this, and you are a little confused about what your body has been going through – make it a priority to speak to someone about this.

One thing that will set you a part as a young lady is learning to effectively communicate your needs and desires at a young age so that no one can come along and take advantage of you. Start now by addressing your feelings before your emotions spin out of control and you lose control of yourself.

>**1.** When you are around boys (any one really) it is extremely important that you assess how you feel. Do you feel safe? Are you allowing words to woo you into doing things you won't feel good about when it's over? Is someone talking to you in a way that makes you feel good but bad at the same time? Are you sure you're okay with the kind of conversation that he is having with you? Always trust your first instinct. Do not EVER talk yourself into feeling okay with the way someone is making you feel if you really feel icky about it. If you feel

scared – LEAVE! If you feel threatened – RUN! If he yells at you – GET AWAY!

You have the right to ALWAYS feel safe. It's a very cliché saying but, "Anger is one letter short of D-anger!" remember that if he ever starts talking to you hard, hitting you, or even looking like he wants to assert his "manliness" and show you "who's in charge!" Get out of that situation right now if you are in it already little sister. If you do not know how to get out of this kind of situation, talk to an adult that you trust. Your life is too precious to be taken away by some boy that never learned to be a man.

Physical abuse is not the only kind of abuse. Do not let someone speak ill of you. Make sure you KNOW who you are so that a man (any person, male or female) can NEVER talk down to you. Emotional abuse is just as damaging as physical abuse. Remember – you are of royal descent. Your father is the King of Kings! You deserve to be treated like royalty. Get your Beautiful self out of any situation that doesn't mirror God's love for you. Get out quick!

2.Your virginity is a gift. Imagine your "special, private place" is wrapped up in a box with a beautiful red bow tied around it. This precious gift is only for one person – your husband. It should only be opened one time so handle this precious cargo with care. Think about who you let touch it and talk to you about it. Be especially careful who you let have it. Because this special gift was designed for only one – there are consequences to sharing it before it is time.

Do not let anyone talk you into sharing this precious gift with them if they are not your husband. Anyone that tries to manipulate you into giving this gift to them is no good for you. He does not respect you and will break your heart. When the time is right, God will send that special person to come find you. After you have legally become husband and wife, then you can share this precious gift with your husband.

Remember, your hormones and emotions are tied together. You may be extremely attracted to someone and you may even feel like you love that person and you want to share your virginity with them but sex will NEVER help you keep someone around that God did not design for you in the first place. Do not be ashamed of the way your body feels when you are attracted to a man – but, be sure to not find yourself too deep into temptation to get out of a situation on your own strength.

3. If you have already had sex, do not be ashamed. I do not have any stones to throw at you little sister. Neither does anyone else, because we ALL have sinned and fallen short of the glory of God. My sin is no better or worse than yours. I am not condoning your sin – all sin has a consequence. But I am here to tell you that if you have already lost your virginity, that's not the end of life with God. Our heavenly father will forgive you if you ask him genuinely for his forgiveness and then turn from your ways. Do not beg God for his forgiveness and then continue to sin over and over again. You must completely turn away from those ways.

If you have already had sex and you are not married, you can practice abstinence. Abstinence is when you decide that you are going to keep yourself from having sexual intercourse again. Abstinence is the only true way to keep yourself from having a child before you are married and it is also the only 100% full proof protection from sexually transmitted disease.

How can you abstain from sex when you've done it already and now the enemy has convinced you that it's too late – you've done it already, you may as well keep doing it? Remember I said wisdom is going to be a major necessity in order to make it through this season of your life. You need to learn to not be where you shouldn't be and be where you should be. Discern each situation and ALWAYS trust your instincts. Ask God to lead you away from temptation and then keep yourself away from situations that will bring about temptation.

4. Possibly none of the above matters to you. Maybe you have decided that you are going to do what you want to do and that's the end of that. Little sister, I warn you against this kind of rebellion. You need to take the advice of a person that struggled for the majority of her adult life with lust. Lust only brings confusion and you will never be satisfied. You think you just want sex with this person that you are so in love with and the next thing you know – you're dealing with masturbation too. You think masturbation is the end of the line and then all of a sudden you find yourself craving porn. You were just having sex with your first love, then the two of you didn't work out so now it's on to #2 sex partner... then #3 sex partner and when you finally come to yourself your number has gotten out of control. Bitterness, shame, guilt will start to haunt you – but the enemy does not let up that easy... he will just lead you further down this path of destruction.

I'm not trying to scare you into obedience. I pray that you will just do what is right, but I am not ignorant to the fact that some of my little sisters will choose to still engage in sexual activity before marriage. The next thing I am going to share with you is not to condone this behavior – but to keep you from getting hurt or ending up in a situation that your young body and mind is not prepared for.

If you are having sex, you need to use protection. If you are not using any type of birth control, please please please speak to your parent or an adult that you trust and learn about your options. Even if you take an oral contraception to prevent pregnancy you must know there are still risks of becoming pregnant and/or contracting an STD. Because of this, it will be best for you to ensure that your sex partner uses a condom. If your sex partner refuses to use a condom – RUN! Do NOT jeopardize your LIFE for a momentary experience of satisfaction.

Devotional #8

Young Black Girl – you've got to know that ABSTINENCE is the thing that pleases God. But a whole generation of girls and women that look just like you are dying from AIDS so it would be ignorant of me to not encourage you to protect yourself should you choose to still have sex even after I've encouraged you in the area of keeping your gift.

There is so much more that I'd like to say about protecting yourself – namely about protecting your emotions, your spirit and your soul – but that is another conversation for you to have with an adult that you trust. I will say this: I have spent so many years in torment over decisions that I made based on my emotions and raging hormones. It wasn't until my sin became utterly sinful to me that I decided to put away those ways. It was not easy. It is something that I have to pray about often. But the guilt and shame that I felt knowing that my actions were contrary to what God said about me was more than I could often bear.

I remember how I got there – it was me letting some boy talk me into something that was confusing to me. I did not feel safe and I knew it was wrong – but I allowed myself to be a victim. This feeling of losing all of my power lead me to feeling ashamed and insecure. Those feelings of insecurity lay dormant in my life for years before they began to manifest in destructive ways. At some point, apparently I began to feel like my body was a sexual tool that I could use to get what I wanted and have who I wanted. Even though men thought I was sexy – one day I realized that I had never seen my adult body as anything BUT sexy. I just wanted to be beautiful for once. A wise sister from my church came to me and called me out on it. She told me that I needed to stop having sex (the Lord clearly revealed this to her) and that God was going to release me from all of the bondage and confusion that I had lived with for years once I did. Who would have thought that so much of my feelings of inadequacy and inferiority would be wrapped up in me having sex? Well it was! I began to cry out to God realizing that I was "good enough" and "worthy" of things that I didn't feel "worthy" or "good enough" for before.

I want you to know that while society tells you that you are just a hyper-sexual play thing, it's really just the enemies' lies and tricks to keep you from your true destiny. You are more than bumping and grind movements. You are NOT that video vixen you see on 106&Park every day. You are very capable of pure and innocent love. You are deserving of the kind of protection that THE man the God has for you will bring one day. You are much more than a collection of notches on some boys' belt. You are better than a $50 bet for your secret space. You are worthy of true love. You will receive that when you are ready. Don't give your special gift away before it's your time. Maybe "Boys Will Be Boys" but it's VERY important for you to know that you are a Lady – Act accordingly!

Dear Lord,

Thank you for delivering me from the place of shame that I lived in for so many years. You have healed my heart and given me back my self respect. You have reminded me of my beauty and my worthiness. Your grace is sufficient and because of your love I know that I am good enough. Please keep my little sisters with this same power. Show them their worth and encourage their hearts with your promise. Let them feel your affection so strong that a man must go through you to get to their hearts.

In Jesus' Name I Pray

Amen

Exercise #8
Boys Will Be Boys

What do you really believe about relationships with boys? On the following lines, write down the things that you have heard boys say to try to get you to go to the next level with them. The next level could be going from holding hands to kissing or from kissing to touching or from touching to having sex.

_____
_____
_____
_____
_____
_____
_____
_____
_____
_____
_____
_____
_____
_____

Now take the time to think about the following statements:

"If you don't have sex with me, we can't be together because I need to have sex."

"A man has needs."

"If I don't get it from you, someone else will give it to me."

"If you love me, you would give me what I'm asking for."

"I'm ready to make love to you, because I love you."

"I will love you more if we can have sex."

"We can go almost all the way and then stop because I can control myself."

"I believe that once we have sex our love will be greater."

"I want to have sex with you to show you how I really feel about you."

Answer the following questions in your journal entry for this chapter. Be honest about what you really believe. Use your honest answers to help you determine whether you are ready for a relationship that is physical. Find an adult you trust to share these thoughts with. Ask for advice on how to handle the things you may be feeling, both physically and emotionally.

Do YOU want to have sex?

If you do, are you really ready for sex?

Are you ready for EVERYTHING that could possibly be a result of having sex?

What could be good about having sex at your age right now?

What could be bad about having sex at your age right now?

If you don't want to have sex, are you considering it because you think he will leave you?

If he leaves you how will that make you feel?

Do you think you would feel worse if you did it and he still left?

Do you think you would feel worse if you did it and then you stayed together?

If you do it once, just because you don't want to lose him, do you think that means he will want it frequently?

Do you think having sex with him will make him love you more?

Do you think having sex with him will make him respect you more?

Do you think having sex with him will make him stay if he really wants to go?

What do you think of him for putting you in this position?

Does this position that he has put you in make you uncomfortable?

Do you respect him?

Do you love him?

Are you friends with him?

Do you think he respects you?

Do you think he loves you?

Do you think he considers you his friend?

Journal Entry #8
Boys Will Be Boys

Daughters of Jerusalem, I charge you by the gazelles and by the does of the field: Do not arouse or awaken love until it so desires." - Song of Songs 2:3-7

Chapter #9
Peer Pressure: Drugs and Alcohol

I had a hard time believing the after school specials that I saw on tv were real when I was growing up. Did popular girls really behave so ruthlessly with their terrible attitudes and their frowned up faces? Were all athletes really that dumb? Could the lesson really be fully learned in a 30 minute episode? I was one of the popular girls in my school, and "no" I never behaved as barbaric as the girls in those movies. I know athletes that scored higher on their SAT's than they did on the court and NO – the lesson can't really be learned in a 30 minute episode. But, apparently the mean popular girl, the dumb jock and the situation where 30 seconds is all you have to choose does exist. The best way to tackle these split second life decisions is to be prepared for them before they come.

Exercise #9

The following are some scenarios that you may face in which you will need to make a split second decision. Write down your responses and then meditate on them so that if these moments ever manifest themselves you will already have a prepared response:

- A friend offers you some marijuana (weed). You are shocked because you didn't know they smoked. You have been going through a stressful time at school and home. They tell you that it makes them get away from the drama in their home and suggest that you try it. What will you say?

- You are invited to a party by the star wide receiver of your school's football team. You are very nervous because you like him so much. He comes to the door of the party with a cup of alcohol in his hand and offers it to you. What will you say?

- The most popular girl in school wants to hang out with you. You think she's really pretty and really smart and would love to get the kind of attention she gets from guys. One day you are at her house and she pulls out some white stuff and sniffs it. She tells you to come try it. What will you do?

- You are leaving an event with a group of friends and you notice that they are acting very weird. You find out from one of them that they are on their way to buy some meth. None of them have ever tried meth but they plan to try it because they heard its better than anything they've ever experienced before. They want you to try too. This is your only ride home. What do you do?

Devotional #9

I made it through high school with out drugs or alcohol being an issue for me. Of course I knew people that smoked weed and drank alcohol, but I had zero interest in participating in that scene. However, college was a different story. My first night at school, before classes even started, I got drunk with a group of friends. It was the most ignorant thing I've ever done I'm sure, and the following day I paid for it big time. I was so sick that my older sisters had to come from out of town to take care of me. I was a mess. I'm convinced that an older guy friend of mine that was there when I was getting drunk, allowed me to go so far to teach me a lesson.

My lesson wasn't quite learned that night because I can count 5 other times between my freshman and sophomore year of college where I drank and quickly became drunk to the point that I was sick for the next few days. I can tell you the exact date of the last time I ever drank alcohol: Saturday, May 10, 2003. I became drunk. I was sick the next day. It was stupid. And I finally decided that not only did I hate being sick for two days after I'd drank myself drunk, but I hated the taste of alcohol.

I can not tell you one good thing about my alcohol drinking experiences, and while my time as a "drinker" was extremely short lived – the one thing that I did learn is that peer pressure isn't always obvious. Sometimes unspoken expectations from friends and associates are the things that get us in trouble. I wish I could take those 6 drunken experiences back. They were a perfect waste of my time and I'm ashamed that I was that silly. However, I encourage you – from my own experiences – to note that not all of your peer pressure is going to be overt and obvious. You must be prepared for how you will respond when the group is thinking for you.

Dear Heavenly Father,

Thank you for your love and protection during the times of my life where I was not making wise decisions. I will never understand why I made those ridiculous choices, but I am glad that you do not hold it against me. Most of all, thank you for the courage that it took to make the right choices. I will forever magnify your name for all that you kept me from. Lord, help my sisters to not "waste" their lives being "wasted!"

In Jesus Name I Pray,

Amen

Journal Entry #9
Peer Pressure: Drugs & Alcohol

"Blessed are those who are persecuted for righteousness' sake, for theirs is the kingdom of heaven. - Matthew 5:10

Chapter #10
Gifts are "Gifts!"

Exercise #10

What are you passionate about?

Once we identify what we are passionate about – then we can have a better understanding of what our "GIFTS" are. And trust me – they aren't called "GIFTS" for no reason! Gifts truly are Gifts! And you should walk in your "giftings" daily or face the possibility of living an unfulfilled black girl life because you didn't choose to BE Who You Are!

What do you think you are good at? Can you sing well? Do you dance well? Do you love art? Do you write well? Are you a good communicator? Do you skateboard masterfully? Do you listen well? What do you think your gifts are?

_____
_____
_____
_____

Do you know that when God created you he was so strategic about your design that he numbered the hairs on your head (Matthew 10:30)? That is amazing to me. It has always been one of my favorite things to think about when I imagine how God thinks of me. I was so important to Him that he took the time out to design me in His own image. He took the time out to get to "know" me so well that he counted the hairs on my head and gave each of them a number. Wow!

If God was this specific about who He was designing me to be   then surely the passions and desires he put inside of me are not happenstance. God personally put the passion for people and art in my DNA. He strategically designed me to LOVE being a "Black Girl." He put a passion in my heart for other "Black Girls." This was not on accident. God took it very serious that I have these desires in my interworking so that when my passion and purpose collided with opportunity – I would have EVERYTHING I needed in order to do what he put me on this earth to do. I believe that part of the reason he put me on this earth at this time, in this place is to empower you into TRUTH! It's my purpose to help you get FREE! And I have several GIFTS that he has blessed me with that help me to be able to do that.

One is writing – hence the reason I'm choosing to put my GIFT to work by writing this book.

Perhaps I should back track a little and tell you that you were put on this earth with a specific purpose. The only 3 things that we will do that is not unique to JUST us is that we were all BORN – we all LIVE and we will all, at some point destined by God – DIE. What is unique about the LIVE part for each of us is what we are doing during that LIVE portion of our destiny.

You are a GIFT to this world little sister. Not only are you gifted but you ARE a gift. You need to spend time daily praying and seeking God to reveal to you what you were designed for. ALL of us were created to bring God glory. We will bring God glory by doing what we were created to do.

Daily Devotional #10
Gifts are Gifts

Philippians 4:13 says that "I can do all things through Christ who strengthens me." As a young girl, I always quoted that and was taught that over and over again until I held it in my heart as one of my earliest bible verses that I had committed to memory. The thing is, I'm not sure if I really believed this until I was an adult. As a matter of fact, it was very recently that I realized that I can literally do ANYTHING that I decide I want to do as long as I do it through Christ Jesus and for Him because He is the one that strengthens me.

I was 25 years old when I realized that I could draw and paint. I woke up one morning and as I cried out to God in my worship and prayer time, I asked him to give me the opportunity to be even more creative for him. I had been writing poetry and short stories and plays since I was a young girl, but I had never thought that I was skilled in the area of visual arts. Until that morning, in my prayer time, I decided that I was going to go buy some canvas and some paint and I was going to paint a picture of a beautiful black skinned girl with an afro.

So I went to the store and purchased paint, canvas, paint brushes and a small art kit that I could mix my acrylic paints on and I went home. I remember that first painting like it was yesterday. I went home and I hung the blank canvas up on the wall as if the painting were already complete. I didn't have an easel so I figured I'd lay some news paper down on the floor underneath where I intended to paint and I got busy painting.

The sister girl that I painted on that canvas made me so proud. Especially when I added her huge red hooped earrings to her ears as I sang along to the music that was playing in the background, I knew that I was offering another gift that was inside of me up to God and that even my painting was the proof that I could do all things through Christ because He gave me the strength to do all of these things.

Now it is my mission to offer up every single gift that is inside of me back to Him. I am very clear that my gifts are presents. They were given to me wrapped in shiny paper and decorated with a big pretty red bow. My life mission has been about recognizing those treasures and unwrapping them to see how God could use them. These gifts were given to me so that I could use them for God's glory. Whether I'm writing a poem, twirling and whirling in a dance, painting a mural or singing a song - I must use each of my gifts to the best of my ability.

God blessed me to be able to do so many things. He has blessed you as well. Make sure that you don't take this precious thing, called a gift (passion and purpose) and hide it underneath your pillow or in your closet. Your gift is a GIFT that keeps giving. You just have to choose to live and live and live! And once you start living... you'll see how much your gift will open up doors for you, bring you peace and make you feel content.

Dear Lord,

Thank you for these gifts that you have given us. Thank you for the gift of life and especially for the gift that is your Son, Jesus Christ. I pray that you will show us how to use our gifts, appreciate our gifts and share our gifts so that we may have happy and full lives and so that you may be blessed by our appreciate of our gifts. I know that we will show you how much we appreciate our gifts by using them and sharing them. Help my little sisters to know that they are special and unique and that their gifts truly are gifts.
In Jesus' Name,

Amen

Journal Entry #10
Gifts Are Gifts

Each man has his own gift from God; one has this gift, another has that.
- 1 Corinthians 7:7

Be The Change

One thing I know for sure is that it takes the whole community to empower itself. I can tell you all day long that you are beautiful and wonderful and awesome and amazing but as soon as you close this book, if your brother or your aunt or even your parents come into your room and tell you something completely different then the struggle to truly grasp the truth of who you are will continue. Then you have society telling you that you should look a certain way; add on to that the reality of music videos and a culture that is extremely focused on sex and nudity; a reality where a long blonde haired size 2 is seen more frequently on your television than an average size 14 woman with brown skin and thick lips.

I say you are beautiful and blessed but you live daily in a culture of people tearing you down and showing you ugly images that do not represent who you really are. Listen! I am not ignorant to these devices. I live in these same communities. The one thing that I am very clear about, however, is that my voice is powerful enough to make the change in my community. I can represent beauty by being myself. I can encourage others by encouraging them through my actions. Do you understand what I'm saying to you? I'm telling you to get ahold of this truth and then "BE THE CHANGE" that your community needs. Because it is going to take the community to empower itself, YOU are going to have to teach the community.

Teaching the community is NOT easy. Some people will tell you that you are doing too much. Some people will try to tear you down and say that the things you believe about yourself are not true. But just remember that you were created in God's image. When He created you He said, "It is VERY good!" NEVER ever let anyone tell you otherwise. In fact, when people try to tell you these ugly things about yourself, tell them that you refuse to accept those untruths and then, in return tell them, "And YOU are VERY wonderfully made as well!"

See... the idea of empowering a community is that you don't have to bear the burden of being great by yourself. You can lift your friends up with you. If they don't want to be great with you, you need to rethink those friendships and choose some friends that want to be great. You can lift your family up with you. While you can't choose new family members, you can be very wise about the conversations that you entertain. If you have family members that put you down, don't walk away from those conversations feeling defeated - try harder to encourage them first, then come back to your journal entries that you have written to yourself to encourage you on days like these.

In order to be empowered and STAY empowered... you have to decide right now, today - that you realize this is a life journey you are on. You are going to have some great days. On these days you are going to want to save the world. You are also, however, going to have some bad days. On these days you are going to want to change everything about yourself. You won't feel pretty. You won't feel encouraged. You won't feel like "you can do all things through Christ who strengthens you." You won't feel good at all. BUT... you are working towards empowering yourself and empowering a community of people that you can support on their bad days and others that will support you on your down days. Either way... you always have your journal to come back to that will remind you of the good things you say and believe about yourself.

I'm proud of you for making it through this book. While these are not ALL of the conversations that you need to be having as a young black girl, this is a start. It is going to be very important for you to find adults that you can trust to have dialogue with. I'm not suggesting this because I think adults have ALL the answers. I'm suggesting you have adults that you can trust and be completely honest with so that you have someone that will give you good advice, based on their experience and life wisdom. Contrary to how smart your best friend from homeroom and first period is, you have to remember that she is still trying to maneuver through life and learn the same way that you are. Finding someone that you trust, that is older than you is a great idea because they can use their experience and love for you when giving you advice and helping you work through the tough decisions that you have to make as a Young Black Girl.

You are going to be well! I know it... Now you just have to decide in your heart that you are committed to the truth about yourself and no matter what, don't let anyone change your mind about these truths - Including You!

About the Author

Ebony Janice Moore is a Self proclaimed "Sista-Girl", artist, activist, community loving friend -She is the author of a book of poems entitled: *Young Black Girl* (belle noire publishing) and *Love Poems for Ivan: and for the times that I hate you* (belle noire publishing); founder of The Free Girl Project (a young women's ministry), has contributed to The Atlanta Tribune magazine, and is a motivational speaker and teacher of the curriculum she designed called - Black Girl Curriculum (which includes her 10 Things Every Black Girl Should Know list).

EbonyJanice works full time as an advocate for Free Girls (www.iamafreegirl.com) and is pursuing her dreams of being free to travel, love and have peace 24 hours a day. She is an artist, animator, creator and painter (www.bneverything.com), an author advocate (www.jesuiswords.com), a creative job and employment blogger (www.totallyandcreativelyemployed.com), and a healthy coffee expert (www.ebonyjanice.organogold.com). She loves photography and thoroughly enjoys spending time with this man that she loves (www.jeremysbestfriend.tumblr.com). Clearly she feels that's noteworthy.

Made in the USA
Middletown, DE
11 January 2021